Alba and the Sunshine

Story by Matt Dawkins

Illustrated by Zoe McCabe

For Issie,

and in memory of Chan,

who will always be our Sunshine.

One morning, in a warm July, a little girl called Alba was born and the Sunshine had never shone so bright or as high.

The Sunshine had existed long before she arrived,
but it was Alba who taught the Sunshine the true meaning of life.

Each and every morning, as little Alba woke,
the Sunshine rose with her
and together they would laugh and play and joke.

Alba was adventurous and explored the world without fear;
the Sunshine lit the way for her and would catch her every tear.

Alba loved going to the park and exploring at the beach.
She would do so alongside the Sunshine, who was there to protect and
guide and teach.

Alba and the Sunshine were as close as two could be,
together they had enough plans to last an eternity.

But eternity isn't promised,
and one night in November the Sunshine felt very weak.
She used the last of her energy to sing little Alba to sleep.

Alba drifted off, knowing she was loved and adored.
She was completely unaware
that the Sunshine shone no more.

Alba woke up without the Sunshine the next morning.
She was oblivious to the fact her world had changed, without any warning.

The weather was cold and dark, and grey clouds filled the sky.
Little Alba saw her family feeling sad and she would often see them cry.

Without the Sunshine warm or near,
Alba's world felt cold,
and she was sometimes filled with fear.

The days felt endless, but the Sunshine had taught Alba to be determined and strong; those around her were filled with comfort when she sang her favourite Sunshine song.

Alba sang and danced- she did it all over the place!

Once again, this magical little ballerina was able to put smiles on everybody's face.

Alba would look back and talk of her adventures in the sun.
She inspired those around her,
and she showed them the world could still be happy and fun.

As winter turned to spring, the days began to feel less cold,
and little Alba had so many adventures and mysteries that were still left
unsolved.

Alba told her friend Sol about all the things she had planned,
and the first thing he did was take her to a beach-
but one without sand.

Sol didn't always get it right, but he did the best he could.
And he promised Alba he would always be right by her side-
on any rocky beach or tough path where she stood.

Alba and Sol took this list of adventures, and they went on the most wonderful of travels.
They looked for dinosaur bones on remote islands and even explored real princess castles.

Alba and Sol missed the Sunshine every single day,
but they would share their special memories
and it would make the Sunshine feel less far away.

They came to learn that it's okay to feel sad at times,
and this should always be allowed.
It's surprising how often the Sunshine can still break through the clouds.

Alba realised that things can sometimes feel hard
and life after change is never quite the same.
But you can still be happy, feel love and say your loved one's name.

The truth is that the Sunshine will never really go.

Even when we can't look at her or see her, we will always feel her glow.

Printed in Great Britain
by Amazon

43001108R00018